Rich Pickings

To Lorraine,
a valued
colleague
and
friend...

Daphne.

Bold Visions in Educational Research

The titles published in this series are listed at *brill.com/bver*

Rich Pickings

*Creative Professional Development Activities
for University Lecturers*

By

Daphne Loads

BRILL

SENSE

LEIDEN | BOSTON

Cover illustration: Painting by Brigid Collins (www.brigidcollins.co.uk), photography by Angus Bremner (www.angusbremner.com)

All chapters in this book have undergone peer review.

The Library of Congress Cataloging-in-Publication Data is available online at http://catalog.loc.gov

Typeface for the Latin, Greek, and Cyrillic scripts: "Brill". See and download: brill.com/brill-typeface.

ISSN 1879-4262
ISBN 978-90-04-38995-3 (paperback)
ISBN 978-90-04-38994-6 (hardback)
ISBN 978-90-04-38996-0 (e-book)

Printed by Printforce, the Netherlands

Contents

Foreword

We often speak of different forms of writing as if they are different animals altogether, and our expectations of what these forms are capable of and how they are appreciated, as well as how they are produced, are very different. We can see these divisions everywhere – in the variation in product design between which different forms are shared (newsprint, book, blog, pamphlet, magazine, television), in the way these forms are organised in libraries or online and in the way they are taught at schools and universities. The separation between 'creative writing' and 'academic writing' feels entrenched at university level, and yet as a *creative* writer myself, I am increasingly drawn to explore the lyric essay, the poetic memoir ... types of writing that defy formal distinctions and allow the writer to employ the best of what each form has to offer – being able to play with language, word placement on the page, thesis and argument, memory, description and imagination. Daphne's own elegantly-composed and carefully considered language posits vital questions to those writing, and perhaps struggling to write, academic papers – why does it feel painful? Why can't it be beautiful? Would it be easier to think through academic writing (the creation of it, the understanding of it) if we approached it like poetry; something difficult but breathtakingly meaningful, a rich art that does not use language like a conveyor belt to deliver ideas but like cocoons opening to release butterflies into sunlight. We are often unaware of the prejudices we have been taught regarding 'serious, difficult academic writing' and 'emotive, aesthetically-obsessed creative writing', and it may be these very prejudices that are causing us to hit blocks when we attempt to generate important contributions to academia.

Academics are under increasing pressures, squeezed between mounting priorities and demands on their time, and this book comes like a caressing hand on a tense shoulder to offer another way in to reading and writing research: taking joy in the music of creation, sculpting our most precious thoughts, and sharing what we've learned in a way that carries each reader with us, deep into our own learning.

J. L. Williams
University of Edinburgh

Acknowledgements

I would like to acknowledge the support of Geoffrey Baines, Brigid Collins, Hazel Christie, Catriona Cunningham, Gill Highet, Velda McCune, Christine Sinclair, Fiona Smart, Raka Tavashmi, Evelien van der Veer, Jolanda Karada, Elaine Wallace and two anonymous reviewers.

Earlier versions of Chapters 3, 5, 7, 8, 14, 16, 18, and 25 appeared in the blog:

Staying Alive: Surviving and thriving in academia:
https://daphneloads.wordpress.com/

Earlier versions of Chapters 8 and 10 appeared in the blog:

Teaching Matters: https://www.ed.ac.uk/staff/teaching-matters/teaching-matters-blog

Earlier versions of Chapters 18, 21, 22, and 23 appeared in the blog:

Inspiring and creative insight into learning and teaching from the Institute for Academic Development at the University of Edinburgh:
https://iad4learnteach.wordpress.com/

Cover Illustration

I am grateful to Kathleen Jamie, for permission to use the cover image. This image was made in response to a collaboration between Kathleen and the artist Brigid Collins in Frissure (Polygon, 2013).

Credits Illustrations

Geoffrey Baines is a freelance futures-mentor, blogger and doodler; he also works part-time with the University of Edinburgh's Chaplaincy making this work available to both students and staff.

For 2014, Geoffrey set himself the challenge of blogging every day for a year but wanted some degree of difficulty. Only allowing himself to post his daily blog if he added a doodle provided the necessary challenge. Four years later, he continues to blog and doodle every day but the doodling has resulted in recently publishing a mindful colouring book and designing images for corporate and personal use, large and small.

Geoffrey seeks to be a deeper listener, whether listening to a person's story, a customer's illustrative needs, or a text. In the case of *Rich Pickings*, Geoffrey read through my text and allowed different image ideas to present themselves, these were shortlisted in a quick-sketch shortlist from which I chose those to be developed into finished illustrations.

The idea is not to "repeat" the text but to offer something tangential to it.

CHAPTER 1

Introduction

Dear reader,

As I write, I'm trying to picture you in my mind's eye. For some reason I see you wearing a dark blue jumper. I imagine you holding this book in one hand, looking at it a little askance. I may be wrong about the jumper, but I bet I'm right about the askance.

You may have a class or a workshop that you need to run to right now. Perhaps you're wondering if you can get a cheese sandwich before this afternoon's meeting. In any case I bet you don't have much time. I'm going to have to grab your attention.

I've got something for you. It's a puppy.

Sometimes you're presented with arguments. Sometimes you're handed a tool or a conceptual framework. What you're holding in your hand right now is a puppy: a warm, wriggly puppy. It's playful, unruly and hard to keep hold of. It will need attention.

You may be surprised to hear that this pup of a book has a long and distinguished pedigree. Arts-based researchers, therapists of all flavours, educationalists and practitioners have all worked in similar ways.

I'm an academic developer in a university. I've worked in education in some form for nearly 40 years, but my interests in writing and reading and studying go back much further. If I think back to my nine-year-old self, I'm sitting at a table with my feet twisted round the chair-legs and my tongue sticking out of the corner of my mouth. I'm surrounded by coloured pens and pencils and I'm absorbed in the serious task of making marks on a sheet of paper. Fifty years later, and not much has changed. But why this particular set of marks?

With *Rich Pickings* I offer both inspiration and practical advice for academics who want to develop their teaching in ways that go beyond the merely technical, and for the academic developers who support them. I advocate active engagement with literary and non-literary texts as one way of prompting deep thinking about teaching practice and teacher identities. I suggest reading poems, stories, academic papers and policy documents in ways that stay with the physicality of words: how they sound, how they look on the page or the screen, how they feel in the mouth. I invite readers to bring into play associations, allusions, memories and insights and to examine their own ways of meaning making. I ask what all of this means for their development as teachers. These practices may seem alien to colleagues from some academic traditions, but I have seen them flourish wherever there are open minds and enticing texts.

I challenge both academics and academic developers to:
- reject narrowly instrumental approaches to professional development
- bring teachers and teaching into view, in contrast with misguided interpretations of student-centredness that tend to erase them from the picture
- claim back literary writings as a source of wisdom and insight
- trust readers' responses
- reintroduce beauty and joy into university teaching that has come to be perceived as bleak and unfulfilling

Bringing together scholarship and experiential activities, I present an assortment of writings. There are short pieces that take as their starting point a quirk, an insight or a query and are designed to provoke thought and to entertain. There are activities that can be put to use individually or in a group and there are accounts from colleagues who have experienced the activities. Finally, there are more substantial texts, where I make connections with other writing and research. I have not attempted to construct a single, coherent argument but rather to indicate a range of good things to choose from. I encourage you to explore the overlaps and the gaps, "the frayed edges and loose wires" (McBride, 2009, p. 43).

This has been a joyful book to write; I hope it will prove equally joyful to read and to use. Oh and I'm sorry if you find yourself mopping up puddles.

Reference

McBride, Neil. (2009). Poetry cornered. *Times Higher Education, I*(925), 424.

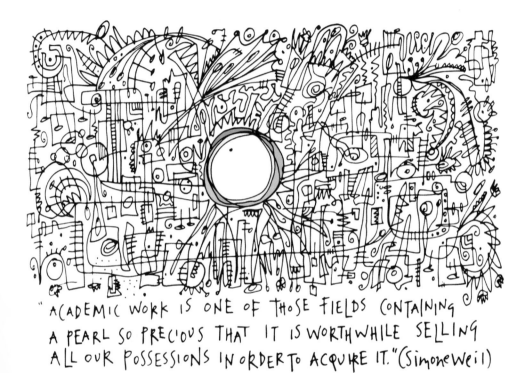

"ACADEMIC WORK IS ONE OF THOSE FIELDS CONTAINING A PEARL SO PRECIOUS THAT IT IS WORTHWHILE SELLING ALL OUR POSSESSIONS IN ORDER TO ACQUIRE IT." (Simone Weil)

CHAPTER 2

Poetry and Policy

Academic staff development, by which I mean the many and varied ways in which university educators learn, change and flourish, is at risk of being denatured by the misapplication of externally-defined standards. This process of denaturing mirrors the tendency to reduce professional learning to a series of predefined, measurable outcomes, with no room for discovery, surprise or critique. In this piece I warn of the risks of standardisation and draw attention to the restorative power of arts-enriched activity as practised in a range of professional development activities. I propose active engagement with poetry, collage, sculpture and other art forms as a way of helping university educators to think and feel deeply about teaching practice and teacher identity. I suggest that arts-enriched activity provides a necessary counterpoint to standards-based development frameworks. Together they may offer release from our incompatible desires for both mystery and mastery.

First, a warning in the form of a poem by Alison Phipps, written during a particularly wearying university strategy meeting:

Policy to Poetry

Transfer the knowledge.
Bank the education.
Roll it out,
roll it out I tell you
across China.
Fill the seven seas
with these words
these my words
and these ways
these my ways.
May all be
competent
efficient
competent
professional
efficient

© KONINKLIJKE BRILL NV, LEIDEN, 2019 | DOI: 10.1163/9789004389960_002

competent
Yes. I repeat. Professional
competent.
It is our settled will
that having settled
our will
we settle for
competence
efficiency
professionalism.
This is the policy.
Ours.
Our policy.
This will deliver.
This will deliver up
a curriculum for excellence,
standards for success.
And across the Seven Seas,
across seven,
there will be
competence between
us. And excellence
and ceaseless
efficiency and
professional success.
And between us
there will be success, I say.
Standards.
Quality.
And of the rolling out
there will be no end.
In place of rest:
efficiency.
In place of beauty:
excellence.
In place of diversity:
national standards.
In place of brokenness
and the tenderness
(which is learning's due):

quality's roar.
In place of dancing:
rolling out.
And there, look, in the
path of the excellent rollers:
violets.
there were [...]
crushed [...]
now [...]
violets.
(Phipps & Saunders, 2009, p. 376)

Phipps reminds us that in our zeal for driving up educational standards we may overlook some precious and vulnerable things that are being destroyed: with regard to academic staff development, I would suggest that these include important aspects of our identities and experiences as teachers. Her sadly funny poem suggests what can happen when our urge to predict, to control and to standardize pushes aside our capabilities for openness, uncertainty and surprise. This conflict recalls what Bakan (1965) identified as the mystery-mastery complex. A complex is a recurrent pattern of feelings and ideas that causes psychological distress. In this case, according to Bakan, the distress arises from trying simultaneously to pursue two incompatible objectives: to honour the *mystery* of the human psyche and to achieve *mastery* of human behaviour. In the psychology of his time, he argued, progress was blocked because the discipline was caught between these two contradictory desires:

> The dynamic associated with the two objectives of mystery and mastery is such that they tend to reinforce each other in spite of the contradiction between them. (p. 189)

Nowadays, it seems that academic development is caught up in a similar complex.

I suggest that practitioners consider integrating an element of mystery into academic development programmes as a necessary counterpoint to those activities that are narrowly instrumental, or that focus on unidirectional conceptual change.

And finally a short piece that I wrote as a companion piece to Alison's. It's a poem of hope.

When Poetry's the Policy

Let's share the not knowing
Bring out the education
Let it unfurl
Wherever
Let's leave out some of the words
Let's unsettle
Let there be understanding between us
And
Rest
Beauty
Differences
Brokenness
Tenderness (which is learning's due)
Dancing
Unfurling
And there will be violets
and roses
and there will be thorns.

References

Bakan, David. (1965). The Mystery-Mastery Complex in Contemporary Psychology. *American Psychologist, 20*(3), 186–191.

Phipps, Alison, & Saunders, Lesley. (2009). The sound of violets: The ethnographic potency of poetry. *Ethnography and Education, 4*(3), 357–387.

CHAPTER 3

A Stupid Way to Eat a Peach

Some academic writing tastes like a mouthful of old socks, and some is very tough indeed; but occasionally I come across a piece so delicious that reading it is like eating peaches. Here, for example, is an extract from one of my favourite writers on learning and teaching, Stephen Rowland:

> Take the following lines from Wordsworth's Prelude (1975 edition lines 360–361) in which he describes his feelings when, as a child, he took a rowing boat out at night and rowed across Lake Windermere towards the mountains on the opposite side of the lake:
>
> > 'It was an act of stealth
> > And troubled pleasure' (Wordsworth [1850] 1975, 360–361)
>
> Viewing the young Wordsworth as a learner, this line captures the quality of his absorption in the learning experience, his own sense of agency in the face of uncertainty and pleasure in the face of danger – which is beyond the scope of positivist language. It is a precise rendering of experience, rigorous in a sense that suggests possibilities for writing about learning. To talk of active learning, study skills, student-centredness or other such technical educational terms in relation to this kind of experience misses the point. It misses the point because such terms cannot contain within them the ambiguity and contradictoriness that are captured in this line of poetry, and that are at the heart of the learning experience ... To cast Wordsworth's act of stealth and troubled pleasure as a learning objective simply makes no sense. It will not submit. (Rowland, 2000, p. 52)

When I invite colleagues to read books and articles about learning and teaching at university, they often get frustrated.
– What's the point of all this verbiage?
– What they took three pages to say I could have said in one sentence.
– Why don't they write in plain English?
So I push them a little, get them to really listen to the words. Some of their responses are wonderful. They might find vampires in threshold concepts (Chapter 18) or bacteria in academic development (Chapter 16).

© KONINKLIJKE BRILL NV, LEIDEN, 2019 | DOI: 10.1163/9789004389960_003

Sometimes it's harder and I watch them struggling to break through layers of language to reach the ideas inside. For them, words are a husk to be discarded; it is meaning that is the nutritious kernel.

Well, I suppose that's a good way to tackle almonds: with a strong nutcracker and gritted teeth. But it's a stupid way to eat a peach.

Acknowledgement

An earlier version of this chapter appeared previously on my blog: "Staying Alive: Surviving and Thriving in Academia" (https://daphneloads.wordpress.com/).

Reference

Rowland, Stephen. (2000). *The enquiring university teacher*. Buckingham: Open University Press.

I wouldn't want to be sitting in the front row for that!
THE PEACHCRACKER
a new twist on a Christmas classic

CHAPTER 4

Close Reading

By 'close reading' I mean paying sustained, careful attention to a short text, word by word and line by line, in order to build up layers of meaning. For colleagues who are new to reading about learning and teaching in higher education I find that this practice offers the possibility of immediate, deep engagement with both literary and non-literary writings in order to gain insight into teaching practice and teacher identities. The focus is on the words on the screen or the page, without the requirement for additional reading.

When we zoom in closely on a short piece of writing, some aspects of the context must, at least temporarily, recede into the background. Critics, writers and teachers of literature have argued passionately for bringing one or more of these aspects back in to full view. Some, for example, remind us of the historical aspects of a text; others warn of the dangers of an (apparently) apolitical reading; some regret the loss of the learned professors with their apercus and footnotes; some redirect us to theory and away from the vagaries of direct experience; others again point out the risk of self-absorbed readings. See Piette (2014) for a wise summary of these arguments.

When I began to use the term "collaborative close reading of teaching texts" to describe work that I was doing with academics who teach (Loads 2013, p. 950), I was largely unaware of this fraught history of the term "close reading." I have learned from these historical debates what we might lose: perspective, history, politics, scholarship, theoretical sophistication or objectivity. However, it is a more recent challenge from the world of digital humanities that has reminded me of exactly what we might gain. Moretti (2013) claims that the analysis of large quantities of writing carried out by sophisticated machines allows us to access data that are too small for humans to notice and too big for us to take in. This "distant reading" works with the extremes of macro and micro, instead of the anthropocentric scale that we are familiar with. It is exactly that human scale that interests me here: neither huge aggregations of texts, nor minute fragmentation of utterances, but particularity of experience and meaning.

I am interested in what happens (and what might happen) when a teacher engages intimately with both literary and non-literary texts as one way of making sense of their teaching practice and teacher identities. My thinking here owes much to reader response theory, since I am interested in the experience of the reader in responding to the text and creating a poem (Rosenblatt, 1995).

© KONINKLIJKE BRILL NV, LEIDEN, 2019 | DOI: 10.1163/9789004389960_004

It is Louise Rosenblatt who drew the distinction between "efferent" and "aesthetic" meanings. The former is the information contained in a text that one can pick up and carry away in the form of instructions for action; the latter is a living through of all the connotations surrounding the words. We might usually expect to read an academic paper for its efferent content and a poem for its aesthetic meanings, but Rosenblatt reminds us that both efferent and aesthetic aspects are a part of every reading. I develop this idea by inviting colleagues to read academic papers and policy documents, usually valued for their efferent potential, as if they were literature, thus giving access to their aesthetic meanings as well.

Like Rosenblatt, I view this as part of a development process that fosters both self-awareness and criticality.

References

Loads. (2013). Collaborative close reading of teaching texts: One way of helping academics to make sense of their practice. *Teaching in Higher Education, 18*(8), 950–958.

Moretti, F. (2013). *Distant reading.* London: Verso.

Piette, A. (2014). Close reading and contemporary poetry. In Peter Robinson (Ed.), *The Oxford handbook of contemporary British and Irish poetry.* Oxford University Press.

Rosenblatt, L. (1995). *Literature as exploration: The reader, the text and the poem.* The Modern Language Association of America.

THE
GLORY
IS IN THE
DETAILS

thinsilence.org

CHAPTER 5

Slow Reading

In my job as an academic developer, I have often encouraged university lecturers to read widely about learning and teaching. These days I'm urging them to read *slowly*. I want them to pay careful attention to a text, word by word, in order to work out what it really means for them. I encourage colleagues to read excerpts from academic papers, policy documents, poems and other writings. I ask them questions about their individual responses:
– What strikes you as surprising or significant about this text/line/word?
– What questions does it raise for you?
– What ambiguities and contradictions are you aware of?
– What resonates with you?
These discussions open up the possibility of spontaneous readings that capture nuances and associations. We then turn to a deeper level of contemplation when I invite them to make judgements about the relevance of their readings. I help participants to make creative connections with their teacher identities and teaching practice:

- So what does this mean for you?
- How can you relate this to something you already understand about your teaching?
- Is there an important idea here that you can use in your thinking?
- Have you ever experienced a situation that sheds light on this idea? (Kain, 1998)

Useful for lecturers, slow reading is also valuable for students. In a series of videos that are at the heart of the Massive Online Open Course, "Modern and Contemporary American poetry," Professor Al Filreis facilitates a group of students in collaborative close readings of US poets including Emily Dickinson, Walt Whitman and Gertrude Stein. Many of the poems are considered "difficult" but Filreis coaxes his students to work together, teasing out a range of meanings, word by word. He likens this slow reading to the slow food movement, and suggests that both can improve our health by aiding our respiration, digestion, sociality and mindfulness.

Students in Professor Jennifer Roberts' (2013) art history classes at Harvard are also encouraged to slow down. She insists that they go to an art gallery and spend three solid hours observing a single painting and noting their own

© KONINKLIJKE BRILL NV, LEIDEN, 2019 | DOI: 10.1163/9789004389960_005

observations before they consult any books or online resources. Although they find the assignment bewildering and even painful, this gives her students insight into the experience of "deceleration, patience and immersive attention." Roberts claims that in a world where everything else is pushing us to speed up and to react to multiple distractions, such contemplative practices teach the value of patience and slowing down. Deceleration is as important for the trained eye as for the novice; she tells how it took her 45 minutes to notice a tiny detail of a painting that contributed to her understanding of its meaning. Nor is a contemplative approach confined to art history: she claims that other disciplines repay patient attention, whether the object is "a star, a sonnet (or) a chromosome."

In her talk, the "Power of Patience," Professor Roberts leaves us with a challenge: if we are to ask our students to make time for "concentrated, slow, non-distracted experiences of learning," how can we find ways to create these experiences in our own lives as educators?

Acknowledgement

An earlier version of this chapter appeared previously on my blog: "Staying Alive: Surviving and Thriving in Academia" (https://daphneloads.wordpress.com/).

References

Filreis, Al. (2013). *Modern and contemporary American poetry.* Retrieved October 10, 2017, from https://www.coursera.org/course/modernpoetry

Kain, Patricia. (1998). *How to do a close reading.* Retrieved October 10, 2017, from http://writingcenter.fas.harvard.edu/pages/how-do-close-reading

Roberts, Jennifer. (2013). *The power of patience: Teaching students the value of deceleration and immersive attention.* Retrieved November 19, 2018 from http://harvardmagazine.com/2013/11/the-power-of-patience

let me reAd
SLOwly

witH my
jouRNal
aNd my
pEn: bLiss

CHAPTER 6

What's the Use of Literature?

It is not unreasonable to assume that research reports and descriptions of teaching practice, even though initially daunting and unfamiliar might help university teachers to a better understanding of their teaching. But what's the use of literature in this situation? What could an academic get out of reading poems or extracts from novels that might help them develop as a teacher? In *The Uses of Literature* (2008) Felski puts forward a convincing case for a more open and generous attitude to what literature has to offer both general and academic readers. Her book is written in sadness at the prevalence of "the hermeneutics of suspicion" – the narrowness of response that has become the norm in literary reading, in which texts are no longer seen as sources of insight or understanding. She also disapproves of the accusations of naivety levelled at the general reader who may look to books for something that helps them to make sense of the world. She regrets that we seem to have lost faith that through reading literature we can "expand, enlarge or reorder our sense of how things are" (p. 83).

In her reassessment of what the reading of literature may offer both the general reader and the academic, Felski suggests four categories of value that literature may have for us: recognition, shock, enchantment and knowledge. It is her concept of "recognition" as an important motivation for reading literature that is of particular relevance here.

This is how she describes the moment of recognition:

> I feel myself summoned, called to account: I cannot help seeing traces of myself in the pages I am reading. Indisputably, something has changed; my perspective has shifted; I see something that I did not see before. (p. 23)

But this recognition can be subtle:

> When we recognise something we literally "know it again"; we make sense of what is unfamiliar by fitting it into an existing scheme. Yet ... recognition is not repetition; it denotes not just the previously known, but the becoming known. Something that may have been sensed in a vague, diffuse, or semi-conscious way now takes on a distinct shape, is amplified, heightened, or made newly visible ... something ... inspires a revised or altered sense of who I am. (p. 25)

© KONINKLIJKE BRILL NV, LEIDEN, 2019 | DOI: 10.1163/9789004389960_006

I have witnessed such acts of recognition as colleagues read together and make sense of their reading. Sometimes they report feeling less alone. Often they see something familiar, sometimes something new and sometimes something that does not yet exist.

Literature is good for thinking with.

Reference

Felski, Rita. (2008). *The uses of literature.* London: Blackwell.

MAKE OF IT
WHAT YOU WILL

thinsilence.org

CHAPTER 7

What Do Academic Developers Do?

I've been an academic developer for several years now and friends and family still ask

What is it you do again?

I usually say that I help academics to improve their teaching. But "develop" is such a slippery word. What exactly does it mean?

A colleague and I recently posed that question to a room full of academic developers (yes, there are a lot of us about). To help them get started we suggested a few analogies.

Are you like property developers, knocking things down and putting up new constructions?

Perhaps you're more like chess players, developing pieces by moving them into powerful positions?

The academic developers weren't very keen on these commercial and managerial images for what they do. They preferred humanistic metaphors, seeing themselves as photographers bringing out latent qualities or gardeners coaxing a barren or overgrown area to fruition. One lively group chose the image of bacteria in a Petri dish. *You can't make colleagues develop, but you can create an environment where they thrive.*

Looking afresh at our job titles was fun, but I had a serious purpose in mind. I wanted to show that the metaphors we choose influence how we think and what we do (Sfard, 1998). An academic developer who thinks of colleagues as chess pieces to be controlled will have a very different approach from one who sees them as diverse plants to be nurtured. And when we stop noticing these metaphors we may unthinkingly perpetuate old beliefs and unquestioned assumptions, making it difficult to introduce fresh insights and critiques of our thinking and practices (Sfard, 1998).

Hidden metaphors can be subtle as well as powerful. By digging into the layers of meaning under the word "development" Webb (1996) unearths the embryo metaphor:

> the idea of development as directed towards a given end and passing through a number of predetermined stages. (p. 64)

© KONINKLIJKE BRILL NV, LEIDEN, 2019 | DOI: 10.1163/9789004389960_007

That idea seems to underlie much of our thinking about learning and teaching. This is an impoverished way of making sense of university lecturers' continuing professional development.

What words about learning, teaching and development do you hear repeatedly?

Which ones seem to you to be slippery or tricky?

What are the metaphors behind them?

What metaphors would you prefer to use?

With thanks to Sam Ellis and colleagues at SHED (Scottish Higher Education Developers)

Acknowledgement

An earlier version of this chapter appeared previously on my blog: "Staying Alive: Surviving and Thriving in Academia" (https://daphneloads.wordpress.com/).

References

Sfard, Anna. (1998). On two metaphors for learning and the dangers of choosing just one. *Educational Researcher, 27*(2), 4–13.

Webb, Graham. (1996). Theories of staff development: Development and understanding. *International Journal for Academic Development, 1*(1), 63–69.

Hey, man, you make my cells divide; you are the petri dish to my ideas
DIVIDED WE GROW
thinsilence.org

CHAPTER 8

You Gotta Have Soul

So what does it take to be a university teacher? This question is often on my mind. I know it's more than subject knowledge plus technique. More and more I'm coming to think that as George Jackson put it, "you gotta have soul."

> Some women, they grow a little shorter,
> Some women grow a little old,
> Short or tall, young or old
> If you wanna love me you gotta have soul.
> (https://www.youtube.com/watch?v=xbcg2hqLznM)

Here Jackson firmly rejects metrics and introduces the notion of soul. Okay, he's talking about love, but I think his ideas apply to teaching too. Seriously. If you want to be a university teacher, you gotta have soul.

So what do I mean by soul? Let me give you an example. Say we're trying to learn about "student engagement." There are lots of ways we could deal with this topic. At one end of the continuum is techno-rational learning. This is like taking the temperature (see Eisner, 1997, p. 7). We could, for example, use learning analytics to find out how many hours students are studying online and how many comments they're posting on a discussion board. This would give us a straightforward measurement of behavioural engagement in a particular course.

If we wanted to delve a bit deeper, we could try to bring about a transformational learning experience, and get lecturers (and students) to re-examine their taken-for-granted assumptions about what engagement actually means. For example, we could consider Mann's (2001) advice to reframe lack of student engagement as alienation that requires from us a response of solidarity and hospitality.

But I'm talking about going further and doing what Dirkx (1997) describes as learning through soul. This symbolic, metaphorical way of learning makes me think of the mythological phoenix, who rises from the flames. One of my favourite ways of inviting in soul, is through collaborative close reading of a poem. As a group, we read and build up layers of meaning, word by word and line by line. Randall Jarrell's piece: "Office Hours 10–11" works well when we're talking about student engagement: https://poetryfeedhe.wordpress.com/2016/11/18/randall-jarrell-office-hours-10-11/

© KONINKLIJKE BRILL NV, LEIDEN, 2019 | DOI: 10.1163/9789004389960_008

Together we could explore the echoes and patterns in this poem: the huntings and hauntings, the poignancy and paradoxes. We could notice that "made to learn" seems to mean both "forced to learn" and "created for learning" and that "we missed you" may or may not have any emotional content. This way of learning can be very powerful; it doesn't, of course, suit everyone.

Techno-rational learning	Transformative learning	Learning through soul
instrumental	meaningful	symbolic, narrative, mythological
adapting to external demands	social critique	spirituality
performance and productivity	authenticity	intuition and emotion
objective report	reflective journal	poem

SOURCE: DEVELOPED FROM DIRKX (1997)

So I think of learning through soul as at one end of a continuum. Techno-rational learning is instrumental; it's about adapting to external requirements. It lends itself to measurements of performance and productivity and can be presented as an objective report. Transformative learning, by contrast, is concerned with seeking and making meaning. It includes not only individual reflection but also social critique. Discovery and authenticity are valued; it might take the form of a reflective journal. Finally, learning through soul draws on narrative, symbol and myth. This kind of learning makes space for spirituality in all its forms; it draws on emotion and intuition. I have given the example of poetry, but in fact soul seems to be at home wherever the varied disciplines we know as the arts and humanities come into play.

And, as George Jackson says:

> You gotta have soul.

Acknowledgement

An earlier version of this chapter appeared previously on my blog: "Staying Alive: Surviving and Thriving in Academia" (https://daphneloads.wordpress.com/) and also on "Teaching Matters" (http://www.teaching-matters-blog.ed.ac.uk).

References

Dirkx, John. (1997). Nurturing soul in adult learning. *New Directions for Adult and Continuing Education, 74*, 79–88.

Eisner, Elliot. (1997). The promise and perils of alternative forms of data representation. *Educational Researcher, 26*(6), 4–10.

Mann, Sarah. (2001). Alternative perspectives on the student experience: Alienation and engagement. *Studies in Higher Education, 26*(1), 7–19.

Wintrop, Julie. (2017). Higher education's panopticon? Learning analytics, ethics and student engagement. *Higher Education Policy, 30*, 87–103.

WE ARE DEEP CALLING TO DEEP

thinsilence.org

CHAPTER 9

Taming the Wild Profusion of Existing Things

I've been thinking a lot lately about putting things in categories and then questioning those categories, and how important both these processes are in learning and teaching. In this spirit I had a look at Borges' taxonomy of animals (in Foucault, 1970) supposedly taken from the Celestial Emporium of Benevolent Knowledge. According to this ancient Chinese encyclopaedia (which almost certainly never existed) animals can be sorted into 14 categories:

- belonging to the emperor
- embalmed
- tame
- sucking pigs
- sirens
- fabulous
- stray dogs
- included in the present classification
- frenzied
- innumerable
- drawn with a very fine camelhair brush
- *et cetera*
- having just broken the water pitcher
- that from a long way off look like flies (p. xvi)

Famously, this crazy categorisation made Foucault (1970) laugh. He liked the way it poked fun at our attempts to "tame the wild profusion of existing things" (p. xvi). It reminds me of two powerful learning and teaching experiences.

Some years I ago I had the chance to study Plantsmanship at the Royal Botanic Garden (RBGE) in Edinburgh: a wonderful course. The time came for us to learn about binary keys for identifying plant specimens in the field. These are a series of questions that enable the identifier to make systematic comparisons between the characteristics of plants. Are the leaves hairy or smooth? If smooth are they lobed or entire? Our lecturers arrived with big bags of assorted biscuits. Our task: to design an identification key that would enable a Martian, or anyone else who happened to be unfamiliar with Jammy Dodgers, Bourbon Fingers and Custard Creams, to identify these crunchy treats. There was a lot of laughter, a lot of crumbs and a lot of learning. More effective than a description or definition of keys, this exercise pushed us into the experience of making decisions about significant differences between groups of objects. It stood us in good stead later when we needed to use keys to make fine distinctions between details in the identification of unfamiliar plant species.

That experience also prepared me for the time when I was teaching an introductory course in Horticulture. My aim was different from the biscuit men. I wanted students to question taken-for-granted ways of classifying plants. I took in armfuls of plant material and asked them to sort it out in a way that made horticultural sense. There were students in the group who had knowledge of basic botany, habitat conservation, Japanese garden design, commercial production of salad crops and herbal medicine. Each of these areas of understanding offered different perspectives on how to make sense of diversity. The ensuing discussions threw light on disputes between botanists who often update plant nomenclature in line with new discoveries, and nurserymen who prefer to stick with traditional names that are familiar to their customers. Students discussed the usefulness of terms like "tender/hardy," "weeds/wildflowers" and "organic/inorganic."

As academics who teach, how can we make use of varied and sometimes conflicting systems of knowledge?

Reference

Foucault, Michel. (1970). *English edition order of things: An archaeology of human sciences.* London: Tavistock.

CHAPTER 10

"Ankle-Deep in Aviation Fuel" or "More Than Violets Knee-Deep"?

Can you recall any times in your life when there was a fundamental shift in the way you made sense of the world and your place in it? Perhaps it was triggered by the birth of a child or the loss of a parent, a change of job, an illness or a return to education? On a less dramatic scale your usual ways of thinking and acting may have been disrupted by a piece of music, a chance encounter with a stranger or a surprising book. Perhaps the transformation was sudden and shocking; perhaps it took the form of a gradual realisation. One thing is clear: you will never be the same again.

This experience is at the heart of Transformative Learning: a concept introduced in the 1990s by Jack Mezirow (1995) that has been explored and debated ever since. It refers to the kind of learning that goes beyond the accumulation of knowledge or the acquisition of skills, and leads to

> a broader awareness of humanity, often of spiritual and ecological dimensions, and one's roles within one's relationships, organizations, community, and world. (Markos & McWhinney, 2003, p. 4)

It is a hopeful way of thinking about learning, based on the belief that human beings can examine old assumptions, dismantle prejudices, question dogma and take action. But it has its limitations. The concept of Transformative Learning has been criticised for its tendency to focus on individual change at the expense of political mobilisation and for privileging the cognitive over the affective. My favourite critique comes from Newman (2013), who laments what he sees as the overuse of the idea in contemporary thinking about adult education:

> Transformative learning still strikes me as inappropriate for the vast amount of learning we do in the practical world. What relevance would it have for a driver learning how to connect a hose from a tanker to a Boeing 787? ... Transformative learning involves self-analysis, and in much instrumental learning there is neither the time nor the need for introspection. No one wants to be standing around on the tarmac, ankle deep in aviation fuel, talking about psycho-cultural assumptions. (p. 2)

© KONINKLIJKE BRILL NV, LEIDEN, 2019 | DOI: 10.1163/9789004389960_010

So how does transformative learning strike you? Is it inappropriate for the learning we do in academia? What relevance does it have for an academic who is learning to teach?

Of course it would be absurdly out of place if our job were simply to connect a hose from a tanker of knowledge to a lecture theatre full of students. But I see it differently. University level teaching is a complex practice embracing knowledge, skill, self-awareness and wisdom. Becoming a good teacher requires a process of development and, sometimes, transformation.

Forty years ago I sat in a sunlit classroom as I was introduced to the poems of Gerard Manley Hopkins. I can still remember the feeling that something very significant was happening (I was right) and the conviction that I would never want to read any other poetry ever again (I was wrong). Particularly I remember our teacher, Mrs. Dyson, telling us about Hopkins' dark struggles with himself and his declaration that because of his faith, his painful life was for him "more than violets knee-deep" (p. 88). That phrase I find at once beautiful and absurd: the clumsy construction seems to show how much it cost him. I don't in any way share his faith, but somewhere between a Victorian clergyman-poet and an oil-tanker driver, I stand as a teacher. Not exactly a technician, but not quite a poet. Neither ankle-deep in aviation fuel, nor more than violets knee-deep.

Acknowledgement

An earlier version of this chapter appeared previously on my blog: "Staying Alive: Surviving and Thriving in Academia" (https://daphneloads.wordpress.com/) and also on "Teaching Matters" (https://www.ed.ac.uk/staff/teaching-matters/teaching-matters-blog).

References

Abbot, Claude Colleer. (Ed.). (1955). *Further letters of Gerard Manley Hopkins*. London: Oxford University Press.

Blaisdell, Bob. (Ed.). (2011). *Selected poems of Gerard Manley Hopkins*. Dover: Dover Publications.

Markos, Laura, & McWhinney, Will. (2003). Auspice. *Journal of Transformative Education, 1*(1).

Mezirow, Jack. (1997). Transformation learning: Theory to practice. *New Directions for Adult and Continuing Education, 74*, 5–12.

Newman, Michael. (2013). Transformative Learning: Mutinous thoughts revisited. *Adult Education Quarterly, 1*(11).

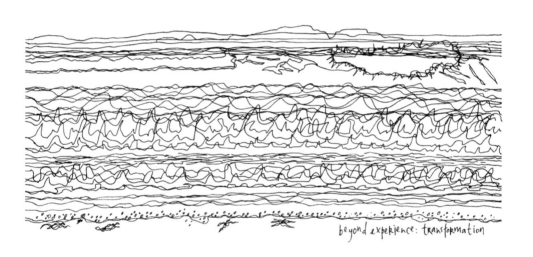

beyond experience: transformation

CHAPTER 11

How to Make a Dadaist Poem
Method of Tristan Tzara

To make a Dadaist poem:
- Take a newspaper.
- Take a pair of scissors.
- Choose an article as long as you are planning to make your poem.
- Cut out the article.
- Then cut out each of the words that make up this article and put them in a bag.
- Shake it gently.
- Then take out the scraps one after the other in the order in which they left the bag.
- Copy conscientiously.
- The poem will be like you.
- And here are you a writer, infinitely original and endowed with a sensibility that is charming though beyond the understanding of the vulgar (Tristan Tzara, 1920).

I love this odd little piece. The calm, instructional style of the poem provokes questions about art and creativity.

"Choose an article as long as you are planning to make your poem." But surely a poem is as long as it needs to be to communicate its meaning? Although many poems are a certain number of lines long (e.g. sonnets), the idea that the length of the poem is the main consideration is amusing.

"Choose." Who has the choice? How much freedom of choice is there?

"Shake it gently." Why gently?

"Copy conscientiously." Such randomness combined with such meticulousness!

"The poem will be like you." Suddenly it's a poem.

So what is a poem?

And what does it have to do with the poet?

And the astonishing statement that "it will be like me." In what ways like me? A combination of chance and pattern? A recycling of other people, other ideas and experiences?

Try it out. And see what happens.

© KONINKLIJKE BRILL NV, LEIDEN, 2019 | DOI: 10.1163/9789004389960_011

Could it be? Her heart sank
as she moved towards
the flurry of paper

Could it be her
ready-to-hand-in dissertation
on Dadaist Poetry?

CHAPTER 12

Etymologies

The beautiful histories meshed inside the roots of words.

TILLMAN, 2011, p. 95

∴

Etymology is the process of exploring changes in the forms and meanings of a word over time and in different contexts. So for example, we can trace the word "text" back to the Latin [*textere*] to weave, and uncover its connections with textiles, texture, context and texting.

Often making these connections brings the same satisfaction as "getting" a pun, solving a crossword clue, being moved by a poem or even gaining an insight in therapy. Etymologising reminds us of both the arbitrariness and the fittingness of words, highlighting patterns and randomness; it can make us laugh out loud or pause to think.

This process of resensitising ourselves to familiar language can be particularly valuable for academics who teach. So much teaching depends on language. Tracing the roots and rhizomes of the words we use can tell us a lot about connotation and denotation. It can revivify dormant or dead metaphors. Seeking out a range of different usages of or connections to words can be illuminating. We may find the cognate to affirm our understanding, to challenge it or deepen it. Sometimes an alternative meaning will be irrelevant: then it will be helpful to tease out the distractors so as to avoid confusion. Sometimes it will suggest a fresh way of thinking about it.

Exploring the etymology of a word is a good place to start thinking about its meanings (see Chapter 16).

Words carry with them the marks of where and how they have been used before, meanings from other times and other contexts.

Choose a word you are in the habit of using.

Look it up in the dictionary.

Pay attention to its origins, archaic uses and specialist meanings.

What do you discover?

© KONINKLIJKE BRILL NV, LEIDEN, 2019 | DOI: 10.1163/9789004389960_012

Reference

Tillman, Lynne. (2011). *Someday this will be funny*. Brooklyn, NY: Red Lemonade.

WORDS ARE
PORTKEYS ...
CHOOSE ONE
AND SEE

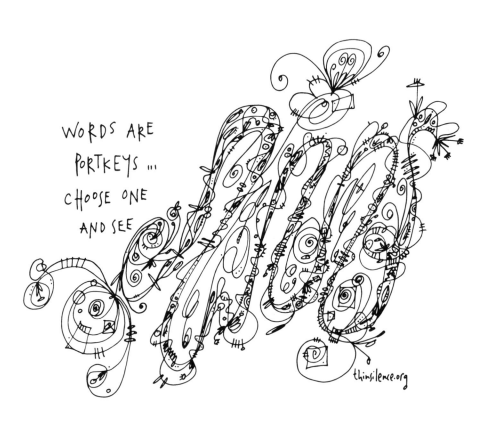

thinsilence.org

CHAPTER 13

Moon

> Last night, when the moon
> slipped into my attic-room
> ... She pretended
> an interest in the bookcase
> ... the books, too, appeared inclined
> to open and confess.
>
> PICADOR, *The Overhaul* (2012)[1]

∴

'Moon' Reading

If you are reading alone:

1. Read the poem out loud, slowly.
   – Read it again.
   – Note down: what did you notice about either the poem or your responses to it?
2. Put the poem aside and write down any words or phrases you remember.
   – Read the poem again, paying attention to the words and phrases you noted.
   – What do you notice now?
3. Play the recording of Kathleen Jamie reading her poem.
   https://www.poetryarchive.org/poem/moon
4. What do you notice now?
5. Here are some things other readers have noticed. What do you make of them?
   – I said, *we're both scarred now*
   – "I read scared instead of scarred."
   – the books, too, appeared inclined to open and confess
   – "the word inclined seems to be a description of a book falling sideways, and then changes, so the book has an intention."
   – "I love the way the string of green beads seem to come to life, like sea creatures."

© KONINKLIJKE BRILL NV, LEIDEN, 2019 | DOI: 10.1163/9789004389960_013

6. What (if anything) does the poem say to you about teaching?
    – Free write for 5 minutes.[2]
    – Read what you have written.
7. Here are some responses from other readers. What do you make of them?
    – "The moon in this poem is the best kind of teacher: she brings everything to life."
    – "This poem recalls for me the moment when a student's interest in reading is awakened. When they go from 'pretending an interest in books' to responding to books as though they were people, with inclinations and things to confess."

If you are facilitating a group reading:
1. Highlight a different word or phrase on each copy of the poem and distribute randomly to the group.
2. Ask a group member to read the poem out loud, slowly. Ask a second group member to read it again.
3. Ask everyone: "What did you notice about either the poem or your responses to it?" Listen carefully to their responses.
4. Play the recording of Kathleen Jamie reading her poem. Ask, "What do you notice now?" Listen.
5. Ask each member to consider the word or phrase highlighted on their copy.
6. Ask,
    – "What strikes you as surprising or significant about this text/line/word?"
    – "What questions does it raise for you?"
    – "What ambiguities and contradictions are you aware of?"
    – "What resonates with you?"
    – Listen.
7. Ask them to free write for 5 minutes on, "What (if anything) does the poem say to you about teaching?" Ask, "What did you discover?" Listen. Share your own responses.

Note

1   The full text of the poem can be found here: https://www.poetryarchive.org/poem/moon
2   In free writing, you write in full sentences, without stopping, on a keyboard or with pen and paper for a set amount of time. Don't stop or go back to correct your writing. The idea is temporarily to turn off the censor in your head.

I am in the moon

The moon
in-between

The moon in me

tinsilence.org

CHAPTER 14

Artefact

> Rona had been nervous about her appointment to see a specialist at the hospital. On her return she was beside herself with worry. "Daphne, they've seen something on my X-rays. They say it's an artefact. Is that serious?"

What image comes to mind as you read the word "artefact"?

Perhaps you imagine a beautiful bowl recovered from an ancient site. To the archaeologist's eye, it reveals its secrets: who made and used it, how they lived and even how they saw the world.

Or maybe you picture an unexpected mass on an X-ray image caused by a heavy hair braid. The informed radiographer sees it for what it is – a potentially misleading anomaly and a reminder that human beings and their technologies are fallible.

Of course you may think of "just a thing."

I like to invite colleagues to create artefacts as a way of exploring ideas words and experiences.

Together we make magazine collages (see Chapter 17), drawings, sculptures or collections of found items that represent our responses to questions: Who am I as a teacher? What am I like as a learner? What does my discipline mean to me?

I suggest that the three common definitions of 'artefact' (a potentially misleading datum, something created by a human being that is of interest to other humans and an unspecified item) reveal a profound differentiation between three approaches to people and experience that are reflected in academic development practices.

The word artefact means made by human skill. The spotlight may fall on the possible positives and qualities of that skill, and the fact that it tells us something about the human being(s) who produced it. Or it may fall on the misleading aspects, the human errors of something that is not natural or genuine but is spurious, misleading, an indication of the limitations of human skill, for example a smear on a slide that is mistaken for a tumour. Finally, it may just be "a thing" with no particular significance attached to it.

So with the art that participants in professional development workshops make (collages, poems, drawings etc.) and with their response to the art of others (Emily Dickinson's poems, for example) there is an emphasis on the positive – what does this tell me about how I am making sense of the world?

© KONINKLIJKE BRILL NV, LEIDEN, 2019 | DOI: 10.1163/9789004389960_014

What does this open up for me in terms of feedback from others? But also on the negative. What does this tell me about the limits of my understanding, the blotches that can be misinterpreted, my usual ways of interpreting that may not be helpful or relevant. Again, does this help me to learn from feedback?

Here's an idea. Go outside for a few minutes. Pick up 2 or 3 objects, for example stones, or leaves (see Chapter 16). Bring them indoors and arrange them on your desk. Look carefully. In what ways does your arrangement resemble you? In what ways is it different from you? What, if anything, have you discovered?

I wonder how you viewed your arrangement? As a thing of beauty, revealing something of the unique human being who chose and arranged the different parts? As a spurious result? As a random selection of things?

Or perhaps you have another way of looking?

Acknowledgement

An earlier version of this chapter appeared previously on my blog: "Staying Alive: Surviving and Thriving in Academia" (https://daphneloads.wordpress.com/).

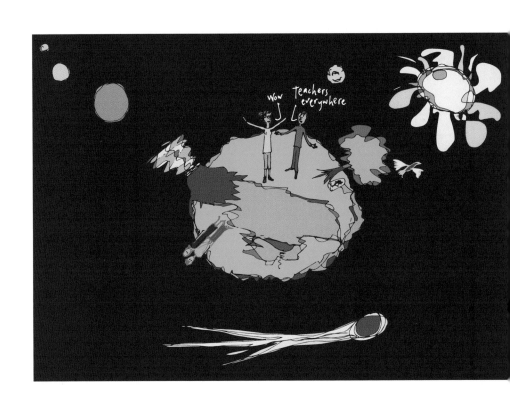

CHAPTER 15

The Possibilities of Human Misunderstanding

The possibilities of human misunderstanding make up indeed a formidable subject for study.

RICHARDS, 1929

∴

Our lovely Latin teacher, Mr. Jones, was disappointed in us: everyone in the class had made the same mistake in our translation paper. On seeing the Latin word for "secretary" we all conjured up a female person with horn-rimmed spectacles (it was the nineteen-seventies). We had forgotten that the Romans allocated jobs differently. We had also forgotten that Latin has masculine and feminine word endings. This secretary was clearly a "he." Well it was clear to Mr. Jones anyway.

Anachronisms are not always so easily cleared up. I remember being enchanted by a line of Anglo-Saxon poetry that described a hand trailing through cold water. I found it very hard to shake off the image of a pale pensive heroine, dipping her fingers in a lake, although I knew that the hand in the poem probably belonged to one of a number of sweating and grunting men and presumably had a big wooden oar in it. The heroine I had brought with me was quite out of place.

In some of the activities in this book, I recommend responding spontaneously to the words on the page or screen, without paying attention to contextual information (see Chapter 4). However, I am aware that by setting up unmediated encounters with unfamiliar texts, we are putting ourselves at risk of inserting ideas into historical writings where they simply do not belong. Not only anachronisms but other blunders become more likely when we read texts out of context. And yet naïve readings can sometimes lead to interesting questions and heightened responses. It can even be argued, and Christopher Ricks (1990) does so with great wit, that the mistaking of words can be a creative act. He describes the police being called to his house in the middle of the night, and his delight when the officer explains that this was because of a report that he (Ricks) had gone "beresk."

© KONINKLIJKE BRILL NV, LEIDEN, 2019 | DOI: 10.1163/9789004389960_015

Beresk! Bereft, burlesque, grotesque, and berserk as I had become, beresk was exactly what I had gone. (p. 461)

When I invite colleagues to engage with unfamiliar texts, like Ricks's police-man they sometimes make mistakes; and like Ricks himself, they sometimes make discoveries, through what he calls a divine dyslexia, or the workings of a co-operative unconscious that allows for inspired errors to be made.

Have you ever mis-read a word or phrase in an academic paper, a policy document, a novel or a short poem?

What did you learn?

References

Richards, Ivor Armstrong. (1929). *Practical criticism: A study of literary judgement*. London: Kegan Paul.

Ricks, Christopher. (1990). Word making and mistaking. In Christopher Ricks & Leonard Michaels (Eds.), *The state of the language: 1990 edition*. London: Faber and Faber.

CHAPTER 16

Random

I often do random things. I don't mean leaving my keys in the 'fridge or flushing my phone down the toilet (although both of these have been known to happen). I'm talking about those times when I purposefully make room for randomness in my teaching and development work.

When I want students or colleagues to engage in new ways with a familiar concept: for example "learning" or "teacher", I present them with a random collection of postcard images and invite them to "pick a card, any card." Then I encourage them to make connections. "What does this image say to you about learning?" "In what ways do you as a teacher resemble this image? In what ways are you different from it?" Time and again I am surprised and delighted by the richness and diversity of their responses. The random images seem to stimulate their meaning making and encourage them to break out of familiar ways of thinking. When one lecturer looked at the picture of Elvis that she had chosen, she became painfully aware of her deep needs for recognition that had been put aside in her cultivation of the "facilitator" persona who fades into the background to allow the student centre-stage (Loads, 2009).

Another favourite activity is collage. I pose a question, such as "What does teaching mean to you?" and invite participants to represent their responses by sticking together pictures torn from magazines.

Having reflected on their artwork, and following feedback from other members of the group, they often notice unexpected juxtapositions or telling details that they had previously overlooked. One colleague was taken aback when it was pointed out to her that the image she had chosen to represent her way up to the mountains of her teaching aspirations was a tiny, rickety step-ladder; there was a long pause while she sat in contemplation of the implications (Loads, 2009). Again, it is the seemingly random elements that give rise to insight.

What is happening here is the opposite of the randomised control trial, where research participants are chosen by a computer programme so as to rule out human biases, conscious or unconscious. Here, the randomisation makes room for human creativity and meaning making.

As academics we are trained to find pattern and create order in a chaotic world. This is as it should be, but just sometimes it's good to let a little randomness into the mix. In the words of Bateson (1979),

Without the random there can be no new thing. (p. 163)

© KONINKLIJKE BRILL NV, LEIDEN, 2019 | DOI: 10.1163/9789004389960_016

Acknowledgement

An earlier version of this chapter appeared previously on my blog: "Staying Alive: Surviving and Thriving in Academia" (https://daphneloads.wordpress.com/).

References

Bateson, Gregory. (1979). *Mind and nature: A necessary unity.* London: Wildwood House.

Loads, Daphne. (2009). Putting ourselves in the picture: Art workshops in the professional development of university educators. *International Journal for Academic Development, 14*(1), 59–67.

WANDERING INTO THE NEW WITH A SINGLE LINE

thinsilence.org

CHAPTER 17

Cut-up and Collage

I love getting people to use collage. I enjoy seeing my colleagues sitting on the floor, surrounded by piles of torn-up magazines and glue-sticks, with bits of paper stuck in their hair. They're so used to trying to grasp ideas and make coherent arguments, that it seems to come as a relief to them physically to take hold of bits of paper and stick them down.

Cut-up and collage are creative processes that have a long tradition in both the visual and the literary arts. From Tristan Tzara's "How to make a Dadaist poem" (see Chapter 10) to Picasso's sticking part of a chair on a canvas; from Bowie's lyrics to Burroughs's novels; from Joe Orton and Kenneth Halliwell vandalising Islington library books to the mysterious book sculptor of Edinburgh, many artists have turned to this form.

Cutting up is a form of analysis that breaks up the item under investigation in unusual ways. This breaking up into unfamiliar sections and the subsequent recombination in unfamiliar configurations can lead to defamiliarisation, the loss or disruption of old understandings and associations and the creation of new ones. Collage is a way of synthesising that involves (mis)appropriating pieces from other contexts in ways that throw up surprising juxtapositions.

The experience of seeing artworks or other artefacts destroyed and new ones emerging can be disturbing. This is not so much because this challenges our sense of an ordered universe, but rather because it reminds us that our perceptions are fragmented and contradictory, even illusory:

> cut-ups replicate what the eye sees during a short walk around the block: a view of a person may be truncated by a passing car, images are reflected in shop windows, all images are cut up and interlaced according to your moving viewpoint. (Cran, 2013, p. 302)

What does collage mean for academic development?

Reference

Cran, Rona. (2013). 'Everything is permitted': William Burroughs' cut-up Novels and European Art. *Comparative American Studies, 11*(3), 300–313.

CHAPTER 18

Kintsugi

One of my favourite New Yorker cartoons shows two disgruntled-looking dogs walking along the road. One says to the other "It's always, 'Sit!' 'Stay!' 'Heel!' – Never 'think', 'innovate,' 'be yourself.'"

Unlike the New Yorker dogs, university teachers are constantly being urged to innovate, innovate, innovate, but this often makes us feel equally disgruntled. We are urged to flip our classrooms, to embrace technology, to make our lectures more interactive, to encourage authenticity in our teaching ... the list goes on and on. Yes, we need new ideas, different ways of doing things, fresh perspectives. But what about the things we already do well, and the things that worked well in the past? Shouldn't we also be conserving, restoring and maintaining, as well as this constant striving for innovation, innovation, innovation?

Quite apart from the risk of overlooking the value of teaching practices and ideas that have stood the test of time, this thoughtless reaching after novelty carries a heavy personal cost. I recently read one colleague's golden rules of teaching, and the first was "never be satisfied." I understand and respect this desire for constant striving for improvement. But there's a recipe for poor mental health if ever I heard one. There's nothing wrong with feeling satisfied with a job well done. When I ask colleagues taking part in professional development activities to reflect on their teaching practice, I make a point of asking them not only what they want to do differently, but also what they want to continue doing. I encourage them to read the educational literatures, not only for new ideas, but also for affirmations of what they already know and understand about what is working well with their teaching.

My good friend Annie introduced me to the concept of Kintsugi. This is the Japanese practice of repairing broken ceramic items using gold and other precious materials, so that the mended parts are displayed and celebrated. This strikes me as a fitting metaphor for academic development and it reminds me of my colleague Heather McQueen (2018) and her notion of "quectures." Quectures consist of a mix of traditional lecturing and peer instruction based around students' own questions. Following a sequence of "Think! Type! Talk!" students pause to reflect on lecture input and then submit and discuss their own questions using the Top Hat audience response system. Importantly, their questions are then re-visited in a future lecture, extending their reflection on the material.

© KONINKLIJKE BRILL NV, LEIDEN, 2019 | DOI: 10.1163/9789004389960_018

The traditional lecture might seem to be broken, but Heather and others are working hard to hold on to what's good while putting it back together in new ways and making their "mending" public. And, importantly, enjoying their successes.

Acknowledgement

An earlier version of this chapter appeared previously on my blog: "Staying Alive: Surviving and Thriving in Academia" (https://daphneloads.wordpress.com/) and also on "Inspiring and Creative Insight into Learning and Teaching from the Institute for Academic Development at the University of Edinburgh" (https://iad4learnteach.wordpress.com/).

Reference

McQueen, Heather & McMillan, Craig. (2018). Personalised constructive learning in lectures. *Active Learning in Higher Education, 18*(1), 11–24. Retrieved from https://doi.org/10.1177/1469787418760325

Why have only questions or lectures when you can have QUECTURES?!

thinsilence.org

CHAPTER 19

Trouble

Academic developers need to communicate persuasively not only with each other, but also with academics from across the arts, humanities, sciences and social sciences. It is a cause for concern that colleagues in other disciplines often find writings on academic development off-putting and incomprehensible. Lecturers participating in the Postgraduate Certificate in Academic Practice sometimes dismiss the readings that I recommend to them as jargon-filled, unconvincing, unrewarding and irrelevant to their needs. For them, the difficulties of engaging with an unfamiliar literature seem to be exacerbated by lack of time, the perceived low status of learning and teaching and their desire for straightforward solutions to pressing problems. Whatever the reasons, it is clear that academics from other disciplines often fail to make connections between "our" literature and their practice.

It is possible (and many of us try) to make our writing more accessible to a wider audience by providing clear explanations of specialist terms, making disciplinary assumptions explicit and avoiding unnecessary ambiguity. This requires a careful focus on the denotations of the words we use – their strict literal definitions stripped of ambiguity and associations. However, denotation is only part of the story. Words always carry with them connotations. This is most obvious in poetry, but applies to all language, including disciplinary terminology. It is important for readers to be sensitive to these additional nuances because they are an integral part of disciplinary discourse.

Looking for Trouble

A case in point is the word 'trouble.' My hunch that there was more trouble than there used to be in the academic literature was borne out by a quick survey. There has been an increase in the occurrence of the term "trouble" and its derivations in three major academic journals over the past twenty years, with a striking "bulge" around 2006, and a slight falling-off in 2010. Increased usage seems to have been accompanied by a shift in connotation. More positive and active examples can be identified alongside negative and passive connotations.

The most common use of the word is in reference to troublesome knowledge (Meyer & Land, 2003) where it is implied that trouble is actually a good thing, characteristic of the kind of unsettling that is required if important learning is to take place.

Peseta's (2007) use of the term ("Troubling our Desires for Research and Writing within the Academic Project") departs further from the dictionary definition of trouble as pain or distress that must either be avoided or suffered. Here it has connotations of agency: it is the practitioner and researcher in academic development who is doing the troubling. What's more, it seems to be an intentional if risky activity – highlighting the role of academic developers as challenging the status quo, stirring up something that is at risk of becoming stagnant, as they create ripples of influence.

Rowland's (2000) allusion to Wordsworth, characterising learning as "acts of stealth and troubled pleasure" also suggests agency and the value of unsettling experiences, while inviting connotations of transgression, thrilling riskiness and the irrepressible (see Chapter 3).

It seems to me that there are three potential benefits to paying attention to the connotations of the terms we use. First we can reduce confusion by eliminating irrelevant associations; secondly we may enrich communication by acknowledging relevant associations; thirdly we might create new meanings by exploring hitherto unacknowledged associations. There is also, of course, the risk of further alienating our audiences, but if this work is done carefully and well, it may be a risk worth taking.

I suggest that we should pay close attention to the connotations of the words we use when writing about learning in order to engage the wider community of colleagues who are concerned with learning and teaching in higher education, and to help them to make creative connections with their practice.

This can be easily achieved by inviting participants to reflect on the myriad associations of the terms they are learning about.

What are some of the connotations of the following?
– Student-centred
– Embedding
– Delivery
– Excellence

References

Meyer, Jan H. F., & Land, Ray. (2003). Threshold concepts and troublesome knowledge 1 – Linkages to ways of thinking and practising. In C. Rust (Ed.), *Improving student learning – Ten years on.* Oxford: OCSLD.

Peseta, Tai. (2007). Troubling our desires for research and writing within the academic project. *International Journal for Academic Development, 12*(1), 15–23.

Rowland, Stephen. (2000). *The enquiring university teacher.* Buckingham: SRHE and OUP.

PLAYFULLY
TROUBLING:

ANOTHER
WAY IN

thinsilence.org

CHAPTER 20

Aleatory Poetry

Aleatory poems are ways of writing poetry that deliberately introduce an element of chance. A poet might, for example, take an existing piece of writing and submit it to chance operations such as deleting every second word, or cutting up the text and putting the pieces together in a random sequence (see Chapter 11).

But chance is a part of poetry in any case:

> Art finds worth in what began as accident. Art has its felicities, to use the good old word which once resisted the exacerbations of the will by acknowledging the part played by hap and happiness in any creative enterprise. (How infelicitous the cagey dicey word aleatory feels in comparison.) (Ricks, 1990, p. 462)

Note Ricks's dodgy allusion to one of the famous names associated with aleatory poetry and music.

Here is an exercise for loosening up and warming up before vigorous thinking. We sometimes start with the quirky and whimsical, and I ask my colleagues:
- "What is the opposite of butter?"
- "What is the opposite of homesickness?"
- Then we might move on to:
- "What is the opposite of learning?"
- "What is the opposite of a teacher?"

By turning terminology around in this way, we bring into view new ways of thinking and seeing.

1. Choose a short text. It can be a poem or an extract from an academic paper or a policy document. The text might or might not be immediately relevant to teaching.
2. Divide the text into individual words or phrases.
3. Identify the opposite of each word or phrase and write them down in order. You can use a thesaurus or work independently.
4. Read the newly-created text. What do you notice? What does it say to you?
5. Swap your text with a colleague. Compare your two versions.
6. What has happened?

© KONINKLIJKE BRILL NV, LEIDEN, 2019 | DOI: 10.1163/9789004389960_020

Reference

Ricks, Christopher. (1990). Word making and mistaking. In Christopher Ricks & Leonard Michaels (Eds.), *The state of the language: 1990 edition.* Faber.

It's her "happen-stance" She never knows which way she'll fall next
THINSILENCE.ORG

CHAPTER 21

Play at Work: On Arts-Enriched Reflection

Hazel Christie

I asked a colleague along to one of my workshops, and this is what she reported back.

∴

An invitation came my way this week from my colleague Daphne Loads. Would I be willing to take part in a workshop on arts-enriched reflection that would involve playing with plasticine? I jumped at the chance, intrigued, along with nine other colleagues from the Institute for Academic Development.

I admit to being puzzled by arts-enriched reflection. I'm not really sure how using the arts can be a ticket to enhancing learning, other than in the arts subjects themselves, but it's a hot topic in learning development at the moment and I was keen to find out more. To my relief, Daphne started proceedings with a definition. For her, arts-enriched reflection is about promoting:

> active engagement with collage, sculpture, poetry, photography and other creative ways of prompting deep thinking about teaching practice and teacher identity.

And play comes into this active engagement. Would we, she asked, think about learning and teaching in different ways if we introduced play to our sessions? Our challenge was to find out. Plasticine in a range of different colours was available to us right from the start of the session and, as Daphne talked, we'd all been busy rolling, moulding, shaping, sniffing and generally abusing it. But now the real work was set to begin. Our task was to produce a sculpture – anything at all – but to be cognisant of the fact that it would say something about us as a person.

Our labours took place amidst much merriment. Various works of art were produced. But things turned more serious when Daphne asked us to reflect on what the sculptures revealed about our identities. And with that the mood of the session changed – the humour now was tinged with vulnerability. But it was time to reflect on how all this sculpting linked to learning and development.

Our next task was to think about 'embedding' which is something we hear a lot about in academic development. Here we were to take an object we had with us, embed it in our plasticine sculpture, and then consider what this might reveal about our learning and teaching.

The embedding exercise was a light bulb moment for me. I'd taken a roll of plasticine and wrapped it around my pen in a spiral twist. And I suddenly got it – I was scaffolding learning. With the aid of structures and supports students can develop more fully as learners and achieve things that were previously impossible, just like my spiral enabled my pen to stand upright which, of course, was not possible beforehand.

But the work didn't stop there. Next we were invited to join up our embedded sculptures to make a diorama. The results were colourful, quirky and, as you can see, really quite inspired. But I had no more light bulb moments, about how all of this connected to learning and teaching.

But help was at hand and Daphne concluded by turning our attention to the theoretical bases of the session. Just what had been the point of all this playing? One explanation was that play acts as a restorative space for academics; it acts as a brake on the excesses of the 'fast university' where there is little time for contemplation or reflection. And what we were doing, she suggested, was a form of embodied learning where we literally grasped at ideas about learning as we manipulated physical objects. So too we re-embodied metaphors, in this case about embedding. How often, Daphne wondered, do we take a concept and use it in a way that is completely disembodied from its original meaning? And finally this example of a 'contemplative pedagogy' takes a stance against the narrow instrumentalism of much of the taught curriculum. Here we were not concerned with targets or learning outcomes but instead were free to pursue an activity that was open-ended and dialogic.

So am I a convert to arts-enriched reflection? Yes and no. I'd happily go to more sessions like this, safe in the knowledge that someone else is creating a learning environment where I can experiment and think outside of the box, and hopefully learn in this embodied and contemplative fashion. But you'll not catch me bringing plasticine to any of my teaching sessions. That's a risky business and one best left to Daphne.

Acknowledgement

An earlier version of this chapter appeared previously on my blog "Inspiring and Creative Insight into Learning and Teaching from the Institute for Academic Development at the University of Edinburgh" (https://iad4learnteach.wordpress.com/).

COLOUR IT

you're
relaxing

DOODLE IT

you're
listening

SKETCHNOTE IT

THE MOON
slip into attics
pretends
makes
books
confess

you're
recording

REPRESENT IT

you're
understanding

MAKE IT

you're
creating

ILLUSTRATE IT

you're
presenting

thisisilene.org

Keep doodling,
Lorraine

Do!

DOODLE
OODLES

CHAPTER 22

Threshold Concepts and the Student-as-Vampire

Amy Burge

I recently encouraged a group of colleagues to think in playful ways about "threshold concepts." Here is one of their responses:

> An academic's life is a busy one – varied, rewarding, challenging, yet often hectic, rushed, and filled with external demands to teach, advise, write, read, assess and talk. In the world of academia, I have found that things which develop us as teachers and researchers – in other words, continuing professional development, or CPD – are often neglected, or hurriedly squashed into a spare half hour here and there.

Well, recently I've been paying a bit more attention to my CPD and this morning I attended a workshop at which we had an extended discussion of 'threshold concepts' based on Glynis Cousins' 2006 article in Planet, 'An introduction to threshold concepts' (article freely available).

To briefly summarise the article, Cousins suggests that rather than 'stuffing' our curriculum with information, what we should do is structure our programmes and courses with a 'less is more' approach centred around 'threshold concepts'. Cousins defines these as key ideas or concepts which are fundamental to understanding the field and which are transformative, often irreversible (once you 'get it,' you are unlikely to forget it) and 'troublesome,' in that it can be challenging and difficult to grasp such a concept, which may seem counter-intuitive.

So far, so clear. However, something that resonated with me during the workshop this morning, was a question we were asked to respond to:

> If we think of learning as crossing a threshold, then it follows that ...

Now, it might be because I've been rewatching *Buffy the Vampire Slayer* this week, however the first answer that sprung to my mind was "it follows that they have been invited in"; in common mythology and popular culture a vampire cannot cross the threshold into a home unless invited.

If the vampire must be invited to cross the threshold, then the person who lives beyond that threshold retains control over who can enter, but once invited, the vampire can come and go as desired.

© AMY BURGE, 2015 | DOI: 10.1163/9789004389960_022

Indulging this metaphor to create an idea of the student-as-vampire, we might suggest that:

– the vampire is (often) an unwelcome guest;
– the vampire will be a temporary guest, as eventually the sun will come up and they will have to leave.

Equally, who invites the vampire in, and why?

As an analogy for teaching, the student-as-vampire is also excluded from crossing the threshold of their own volition: in this scenario, the threshold crossing is a mediated encounter, carried out under surveillance.

What might prevent the student-as-vampire from kicking the door down? What is it that stops a vampire from crossing a threshold uninvited? In the 2008 Swedish vampire film *Let the Right One In* there is a scene where Eli, the little-girl-vampire who lives next door, enters Oskar's home without permission and proceeds to start bleeding violently (warning: contains blood). Does the student-as-vampire experience threshold crossing in a similarly violent way?

So the student-as-vampire who is invited in does not have control over their crossing and does not belong in whatever is beyond the threshold. Yet, equally, the student-as-vampire who crosses the threshold without an invitation encounters violence and possible pain and are equally not at home beyond that threshold.

So, is the manner of crossing the threshold less important that what actually happens or what actually is on the other side? Whether you are invited or not does not seem to make a huge difference to whether the student-as-vampire belongs: they are equally 'unbelonging' in both scenarios.

To make the student-as-vampire feel welcome, we need to 'vampirize' the space; we need to fit shutters or blinds and install a few coffins, making the vampire far more likely to feel at home and to stick around.

So rather than changing the student and de-vampiring them, perhaps we need to change what is beyond the threshold to fit the student as they are. And the point of entry needs to be equally shared or owned by both vampire and teacher so that the student-as-vampire can take ownership over the reason why they are there.

The student-as-vampire must be:

– not invited, but welcomed
– not a guest, but a resident
– what comes beyond the threshold must not be pre-defined, but flexible, adaptable and customisable.

Now, this is a playful analogy (and please note that I am not suggesting that students are in any way vampires!). But it did make me think a little more about how we incorporate or make use of threshold concepts in our teaching. For a start, why do we want students to cross this threshold? What is in it for them and how can we give them ownership and belonging in what lies beyond? What are the problems in the teacher controlling the threshold? Can students take ownership over the threshold and let *themselves* in?

In terms of threshold concepts and the way we design our teaching, perhaps we need to think less about letting the right one in, and more about letting the one in *right* (or right for them).

Acknowledgement

An earlier version of this chapter appeared previously on my blog "Inspiring and Creative Insight into Learning and Teaching from the Institute for Academic Development at the University of Edinburgh" (https://iad4learnteach.wordpress.com/).

Reference

Cousin, Glynis. (2006). An introduction to threshold concepts. *Planet, 17,* 4–5.

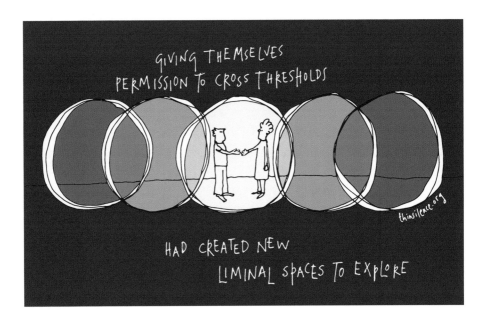

CHAPTER 23

Revisiting Deep and Surface Reading

When it comes to thinking about reading at university we often rely on easy oppositions between deep and surface approaches. Deep is good, surface is bad, the logic goes. And the language sucks us in. Surely we want to promote the kind of deep reading that leads to in-depth reflection and analysis? And to discourage the superficial reasoning and shallow thinking that comes with surface reading? This idea is everywhere. We warn each other not to judge a book by its cover. We tell our students to read for meaning and understanding and not to get too hung up on the individual words and sentences.

However, like all metaphors, this one has its limitations. It can lead us to think of the linguistic features of a text – things like the choice of vocabulary or the rhythm of the phrasing – as being on the surface, and therefore unworthy of our attention. After all, the real meaning lies beneath, doesn't it? Reading becomes a matter of getting through layers of language to reach the ideas inside. We rush to remove and discard the packaging in order to get at the contents. Words are merely the husk; meaning is the nutritious kernel.

But, of course, it's not that simple. The words a writer chooses are part and parcel of what they say. This applies to academic papers and policy documents, just as it does to poems and novels. For this reason, sometimes it's worth taking time to linger on the surface of a text, appreciating the play of light and shade, the colours and textures of words, the reflections that bounce off their forms. Take, for example, this extract from an academic paper. In it, the writer talks about her difficulties in finding a way of incorporating the self into research that is somehow found or revealed through writing:

> This trouble started when I began searching in earnest for a methodological framework that encouraged me to write richly of my experience as an academic developer, as itself an act of research. Indeed, I was seeking both a scholarly argument and a turn to writing that might value this 'self-knowledge' of its own accord, neither as a contaminant to that disciplinary academic *Other* (Krieger, 1991), nor a supplement to it, nor an escape from it. I found autoethnography late one evening in the quiet of the university library. (Peseta, 2007, p. 16)

Notice how the writer's words act out her meanings. The first two sentences show us the trouble that she is in. Caught up in thickly-matted phrases, she

© KONINKLIJKE BRILL NV, LEIDEN, 2019 | DOI: 10.1163/9789004389960_023

hardly knows which way to turn. She seems to lose herself between the two repeats of "as." It seems unlikely that any framework will offer her the encouragement she is looking for. Her appeals to traditional authority in the italicised *Other,* and the reference to Krieger, lend her no support. Then, just as the word "escape" appears, she manages to slip away. That third sentence comes as a relief: she has found a way through.

It may seem strange to dwell on the surface of academic writing in this way. Such close reading has its place in literary studies, perhaps, but not in the reading of journal articles? And yet it seems to me that when we pay due attention to language, the surface/deep binary melts away. By re-engaging fully with the texts we read, we can discover fresh insights and ask important questions. The extract above helps me to think about the nature of academic writing. Why is it such a struggle? And that in turn leads me to think more carefully about reading. Who am I as a reader? Where do I focus my attention? What is my contribution to meaning? And what light do these questions shed on Marton and Saljo's famous distinction between deep- and surface-level approaches to learning?

Acknowledgement

An earlier version of this chapter appeared previously on my blog "Inspiring and Creative Insight into Learning and Teaching from the Institute for Academic Development at the University of Edinburgh" (https://iad4learnteach.wordpress.com/).

References

Marton, Ference, & Saljo, Roger. (1976). On qualitative differences in learning: 1 – Outcome and process. *British Journal of Educational Psychology, 46*(1), 4–11.
Peseta, Tai. (2007). Troubling our desires for research and writing within the academic development project. *International Journal for Academic Development, 12*(1), 15–23.

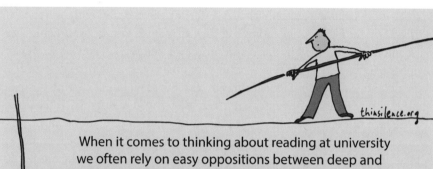

When it comes to thinking about reading at university
we often rely on easy oppositions between deep and
surface approaches. Deep is good, surface is bad, the
logic goes. And the language sucks us in. Surely we
want to promote the kind of deep reading that leads
to in-depth reflection and analysis? And to discourage
the superficial reasoning and shallow thinking that
comes with surface reading? The idea is everywhere.
We warn each other not to judge a book by its cover.
We tell our students to read for meaning and understanding and not to get too hung up on the individual
words and sentences.

CHAPTER 24

The Power of Anecdotes

An early career researcher complained to me recently that much of what we know about learning and teaching in higher education is "merely anecdotal." A senior colleague often prefaces the telling of funny and insightful stories with the apology that he might be "slipping into his anecdotage."

Why are we so disparaging of anecdotes? The word comes from the Greek [a-necdote] meaning "unpublished." It doesn't mean "inherently unreliable" "trivial" or "unfit for publication." In fact anecdotes can be a valuable way of communicating insight and wisdom. I once heard a keynote by Professor Graham Gibbs which consisted entirely of anecdotes: a lifetime of practice, research and scholarship in learning and teaching laid out in a string of small polished pieces, each prefaced with "Let me tell you a story ...." Unabashed in the face of critics who have questioned the authenticity of his anecdotes, that seem to change over time and to fit whatever point he may be making, he cheerfully described his practice as "creative non-fiction." Yes, the stories do change, he explained, because times change and we need to say and to hear new things.

It was inspirational. So here are 7 reasons why I love anecdotes:

- *They're short.* And that's welcome when we're all drowning in information.
- *They're often funny.* When did you last laugh with delight at an academic paper?
- *They're particular.* But touch on the universal.
- *They're personal.* They're told from one person's perspective and can be interpreted from another.
- *They're memorable.* They often turn on a striking word or phrase or a surprising juxtaposition.
- *They distil insights.* The best anecdotes replicate a moment of understanding or recognition with every retelling.
- *They don't even have to be true.* But the best anecdotes have the ring of truth about them, in the way that novels do.

My dad used to tell the story of a verger (a church caretaker) in the village where he grew up, who had been sacked by the ruthless new vicar because he was illiterate. The poor man had no other source of income and was forced to sell small items door-to-door from a wheelbarrow. He did well, and saved enough to buy a van and then a shop. Ten years later, by then a successful businessman, he was interviewed for the local newspaper. "You've achieved so

© KONINKLIJKE BRILL NV, LEIDEN, 2019 | DOI: 10.1163/9789004389960_024

much!" gushed the reporter "Just think where you'd be now if you could read and write!"

"I know exactly where I'd be," came the quick response. "I'd still be a verger in the village church."

In a group, take turns to tell a favourite anecdote about learning and teaching.
– What do you take from each?
– What might change in the re-telling?

THAT REMINDS
ME OF A STORY

thinsilence.org

CHAPTER 25

A Symposium and a Song

What does the term 'neoliberal university' mean to you? I understand it as an accusation that 'the market' is now at the heart of many institutions, with no regard for other values that have been displaced or ruled out. So all around us we see less public funding for higher education, more precarious working conditions for early career academics, less attention paid to student development than to income generation, an emphasis on measurable targets and less kindness and collegiality amongst us all.

Two very different forms of communication have helped me to think about the neoliberal university: one was an academic symposium; the other was an old song.

Some time ago I attended a symposium at the University of Edinburgh entitled Critical Pedagogies: Equality and Diversity in a Changing Institution (2013). There were some impressive speakers. Heidi Sofia Mirza reminded us that, immense and immoveable as the neoliberal university may seem to be, it's not impregnable. She asked us to think about how we can navigate the cracks in the monolith. She warned of the insidiousness of Equality and Diversity discourses with their bureaucratisation, targets, audits and documentation that seem to 'remove Equality and Diversity from struggle.' She offered hope of escape through ways of being that 'decolonise the mind' – reconnecting with sensory and emotional experience and memory. Joyce Canaan's starting point was that those of us who teach in universities have a role in challenging neoliberal values. She reminded us that there is no such thing as a neutral education and that to deny this is in itself a political statement.

And then there's the song. For some time, now, I've found myself humming (and, embarrassingly, sometimes singing out loud) a song from the 60s: 'Twenty-mile zone.' Dory Previn sings about a woman who is stopped by a policeman and is accused of 'screaming, all alone, in her car, in a twenty-mile zone.' I think this hilarious, sad and ultimately life-affirming song is about a human being expressing her fears and refusing to submit to meaningless restrictions. It's also about the person who tries to enforce those restrictions, unaware that he's afraid and screaming too – at his sports games, in his wars, with his police siren. Both within and outside the dominant discourse, they are 'screaming together alone.' Is it too fanciful to suggest that this is what happens in the neoliberal university? Some of us enforcing the rules, some of us trying to break out, all of us feeling like screaming?

© KONINKLIJKE BRILL NV, LEIDEN, 2019 | DOI: 10.1163/9789004389960_025

The symposium got me thinking. But it's the song that I keep coming back to, wondering what it means for me, my colleagues and our students.

Acknowledgement

An earlier version of this chapter appeared previously on my blog: "Staying Alive: Surviving and Thriving in Academia" (https://daphneloads.wordpress.com/).

CHAPTER 26

Envoi

I wonder what you have made of this little book? Have you already read it, or have you just turned to the back, to find out where it's going?

In any case I hope that you will take with you a sense of what it feels like when a piece of writing (or an image or an object) resonates with you, and seems to touch on an aspect of your life. Hidden away in a poem written by Alexander Pope in 1732, I found a description of what it often feels like for me. An Essay on Man seeks to justify the ways of God to man, and along the way lays out some perplexing and (to modern ears) downright offensive opinions. But at one point, the speaker exclaims:

> The spider's touch, how exquisitely fine!
> Feels at each thread, and lives along the line (p. 34)

When I've recovered from that creepy spider's touch, I notice the elongated 'EXquiSITely' (not 'exQUIsitely', as in the familiar modern pronunciation) but 'EXquiSITely fine,' as the rhythm of the line pushes me to pronounce it, stretching out my antennae as I go.

'Feels at' suggests to me a kind of groping – not the assured directness of 'feels each thread' nor a purposeful 'feels for each thread.' 'Feels at each thread' brings to mind both a bit of unfocused antenna-waving, and a careful stopping at every node in turn. Then comes the fluid, pulsing 'lives along the line.' That's exactly what it feels like to me to fumble a little and try hard to make sense of the words and then all of a sudden the slight buzz in 'lives' and the pulsing motion of 'lives along the line' suggests to me the thrill of electricity.

Words are not containers for meaning, or rather not only containers. Perhaps we should shout it in capital letters as do the brilliant Lakoff and Johnston whenever they draw attention to a conceptual metaphor: WORDS ARE NOT (ONLY) CONTAINERS FOR MEANING. And when they are, they are leaky and see-through and prone to collapse. Words come to us with etymological connections to previous times and different contexts, and trailing long strings of connotations that won't fold up neatly into a box. In this book, I've been inviting you, like Pope's spider, to feel at each thread and live (feel that pulse!) along the line. The line may lead you to many places. In this case I've suggested it may lead you to aspects of your life as a university teacher.

You may have other ideas.

© KONINKLIJKE BRILL NV, LEIDEN, 2019 | DOI: 10.1163/9789004389960_026

References

Lakoff, G., & Johnston, M. (2003). *Metaphors we live* (2nd ed.). Chicago, IL: University of Chicago Press.

Pope, A. (1751). *An essay on man, in four epistles*. Edinburgh: James Reid.